FRAG doch mal ...

Bildwörterbuch

Deutsch
Englisch

XENOS

Dieses Buch gehört:

This book belongs to:

ISBN 978-3-8212-2813-6

Verantwortlich für diese Ausgabe:
© XENOS Verlagsgesellschaft mbH
Am Hehsel 40, 22339 Hamburg

Illustration: Günter Phiesel, Klaus Henkelmann
Konzept, Text: Birgit Rehaag
Übersetzung: Frauke Watson
Grafische Gestaltung, Satz: Gerlinde Conrad

Printed in Italy

Inhalt
Contents

Die Maus und ihre Freunde
The Mouse and its friends

Die Maus und ihre Freunde machen gern Musik.

The Mouse loves to play music with its friends.

Was machen sie?
What are they doing?

Die Maus fängt Schmetterlinge.

The Mouse is catching butterflies.

Die Maus und ihre Freunde fahren mit dem Floß.

The Mouse and its friends are floating on a raft.

Die Ente und der Elefant pflücken Blumen.

The Duck and the Elephant are picking flowers.

Die Maus, der Elefant und die Ente bauen Schneemänner.

The Mouse, the Elephant and the Duck are building snowmen.

Die Maus und der Elefant grillen.

The Mouse and the Elephant are having a barbecue.

Die Maus, der Elefant und die Ente spielen Fußball.

The Mouse, the Elephant and the Duck are playing soccer.

Die Ente schwimmt.

The Duck is swimming.

Die Maus packt ihren Rucksack

The Mouse is packing its rucksack

die Trinkflasche
flask

die Mütze
woolly hat

das Butterbrot
sandwich

die Birne
pear

der Schal
scarf

der Rucksack
rucksack

der Handschuh
glove

der Brustbeutel
pouch

der Teddybär
teddy bear

Die Maus packt ihren Rucksack für den Kindergarten. Hilf ihr dabei!

The Mouse is packing its rucksack for nursery. Come and help!

Wo ist der Ball?

Where is the ball?

Der Elefant hat den Ball verschossen. Kannst du ihn finden? Male das Bild bunt aus!

The Elephant has kicked the ball away. Can you find it? Colour the picture!

Lösung: Der Ball ist unter der Rutsche.
Answer: The ball is under the slide.

Im Badezimmer
In the bathroom

die Lampe
lamp

der Abfalleimer
bin

das Handtuch
towel

der Wasserhahn
tap

das Parfum
perfume

der Spiegel
mirror

das Waschbecken
washbasin

Zähle mit der Maus!

Counting with the Mouse!

1

eins

one

6

sechs

six

2

zwei

two

7

sieben

seven

3

drei

three

8

acht

eight

4

vier

four

9

neun

nine

5

fünf

five

10

zehn

ten

Die Ente zählt gern.
Hilfst du ihr?

The Duck loves to count. Can you help it?

Auf wie vielen Kissen schläft der Elefant?

On how many pillows does the Elephant sleep?

Lösung: sechs.
Answer: six.

Wie viele Orangenscheiben sind auf dem Teller?

How many orange slices are on the plate?

Lösung: acht.
Answer: eight.

Wie viele Wolken sehen die Maus, der Elefant und die Ente?

How many clouds do the Mouse, the Elephant and the Duck see?

Lösung: vier.
Answer: four.

Wie viele Sterne stehen am Himmel?

How many stars are in the sky?

Lösung: sieben.
Answer: seven.

Auf dem Spielplatz
At the playground

das Förmchen
sand mould
die Schaufel
shovel
die Sandkiste
sand box
der Besen
broom
der Eimer
bucket
der Roller
scooter

In der Küche
In the kitchen

der Teller
plate

die Gabel
fork

die Milch
milk

der Kuchen
cake

die Kartoffel
potato

das Brot
bread

die Butter
butter

die Gurke
cucumber

die Marmelade
jam

der Honig
honey

das Ei
egg

die Banane
banana

das Messer
knife

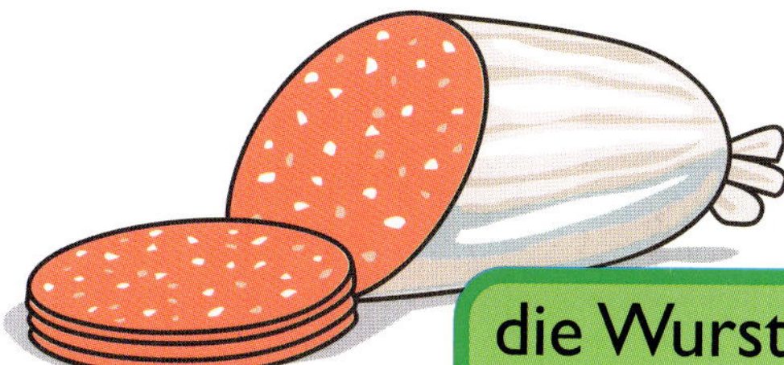

die Wurst
sausage

die Kirsche
cherry

die Karotte
carrot

die Tomate
tomato

das Hühnerbein
chicken leg

der Apfel
apple

die Ananas
pineapple

die Spaghetti
spaghetti

der Käse
cheese

Gräten
fish bones

Wo bist du?

Where are you?

Die Maus steht neben dem Tisch.

The Mouse is standing next to the table.

Die Maus ist auf der Leiter.

The Mouse is on the ladder.

Der Elefant versteckt sich hinter dem Baum.

The Elephant is hiding behind the tree.

Die Ente sitzt zwischen der Maus und dem Elefanten.

The Duck is sitting between the Mouse and the Elephant.

Der Elefant schläft unter dem Bett.

The Elephant is sleeping under the bed.

Die Ente, die Maus und der Elefant warten vor dem Kindergarten.

The Duck, the Mouse and the Elephant are waiting in front of the nursery.

Tiere
Animals

die Katze
cat

der Adler
eagle

der Hamster
hamster

der Affe
monkey

Die Maus hat Tierbilder mitgebracht. Kennst du die Tiere?

The Mouse has brought pictures of animals. Do you know the animals?

die Ameise
ant

der Hase
hare

der Fisch
fish

das Nashorn
rhinoceros

der Hund
dog

das Nilpferd
hippopotamus

Spaß beim Sport
Having fun with sports

Ski
ski

Die Maus und ihre Freunde laufen Ski.
The Mouse and its friends are skiing.

Golf
golf

Die Maus spielt Golf.
The Mouse is playing golf.

Weitspringen
long jump

Lösung: Die Maus ist am weitesten gesprungen.
Answer: The Mouse jumped the farthest.

Wer ist am weitesten gesprungen?
Who jumped the farthest?

Judo
judo

Die Maus lernt Judo.

The Mouse is learning how to do judo.

Schwebebalken
balance beam

Die Maus turnt auf dem Schwebebalken.

The Mouse is exercising on the balance beam.

Maus, Elefant und Ente trainieren Basketball. Wer gewinnt?

The Mouse, the Elephant and the Duck are playing basketball. Who will win?

Basketball
basketball

Ringe
rings

Für die Übungen an den Ringen braucht die Maus viel Kraft.

The Mouse needs lots of strength on the rings.

Folge den Linien!

Follow the lines!

Was haben die Maus, der Elefant und die Ente geangelt? Folge den Linien und finde es heraus!

What did the Mouse, the Duck and the Elephant catch? Follow the lines and find out!

Lösung: Die Maus hat den Schuh geangelt, die Ente den Autoreifen und der Elefant den Fisch.

Answer: The Mouse caught the shoe, the Duck the car tire and the Elephant the fish.

Beim Picknick
At the picnic

der Pilz
mushroom

die Wiese
meadow

das Glas
glass

der Kuchen
cake

das Meterbrot
bread stick

die Flasche
bottle

der Korb
basket

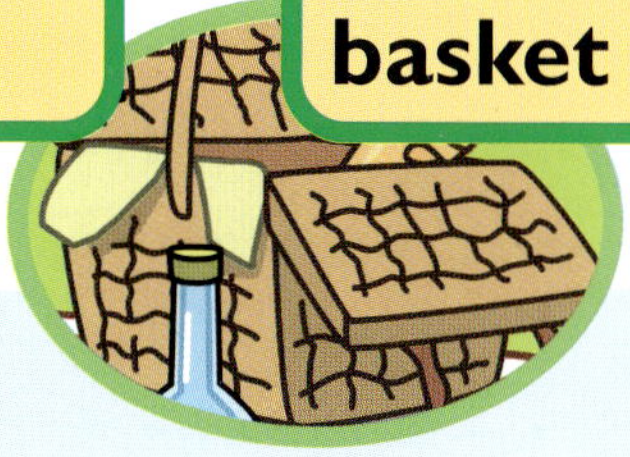

die Decke
blanket

Die Maus, der Elefant und die Ente machen ein Picknick.

The Mouse, the Elephant and the Duck are having a picnic.

Die Jahreszeiten
The seasons

Februar
February

Januar
January

Dezember
December

der Winter
winter

November
November

der Herbst
autumn

Oktober
October

September
September

März
March

April
April

Mai
May

der Frühling
spring

der Sommer
summer

Juni
June

Juli
July

August
August

Im Garten
In the garden

der Rasen
lawn

der Rasenmäher
lawnmower

die Gießkanne
watering can

die Blume
flower

Die Maus und ihre Freunde machen Gartenarbeit.

The Mouse and its friends are working in the garden.

der Baum
tree

das Blatt
leaf

der Ast
branch

der Vogel
bird

die Vogelscheuche
scarecrow

das Beet
flower bed

der Spaten
spade

der Blumentopf
flower pot

Die Maus und ihre Freunde pflanzen Blumen.

The Mouse and its friends are planting some flowers.

Finde die Unterschiede!

Spot the differences!

der Ritter
knight

die Rüstung
armour

das Schwert
sword

der Schild
shield

der Luftballon
balloon

der Clown
clown

das Huhn
chicken

das Krokodil
crocodile

Die Maus und ihre Freunde haben sich verkleidet. Findest du die zehn Unterschiede in den beiden Bildern?

The Mouse and its friends have been dressing up. Can you spot the ten differences between the two pictures?

Lösung:
Answer:

Was machst du gern?
What do you like to do?

Die Maus angelt gern.

The Mouse likes to go fishing.

Die Ente spielt gern mit der Spielzeug-Eisenbahn.

The Duck likes to play with the toy train.

Der Elefant hört gern Musik.

The Elephant likes to listen to music.

Die Maus und der Elefant musizieren gern.

The Mouse and the Elephant like to play music.

Die Maus taucht gern.

The Mouse likes to go diving.

Die Maus liest gern.

The Mouse likes to read.

Der Elefant zaubert gern.

The Elephant likes to do magic tricks.

Was machst du gern?

What do you like to do?

....

Im Schwimmbad

At the swimming pool

die Uhr
clock

der Rettungsring
rescue ring

die Leiter
ladder

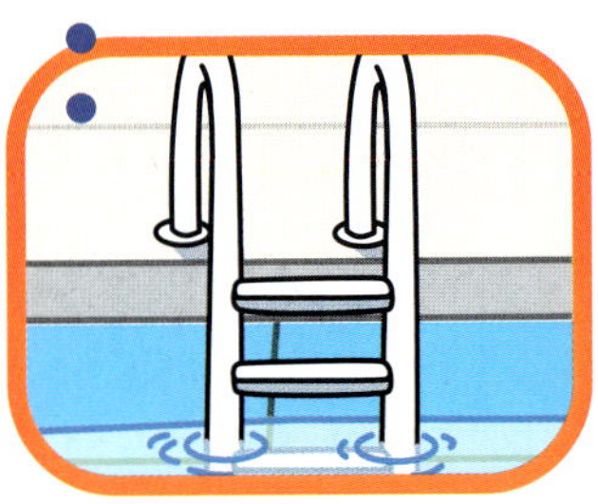

die Quietsche-Ente
rubber duck

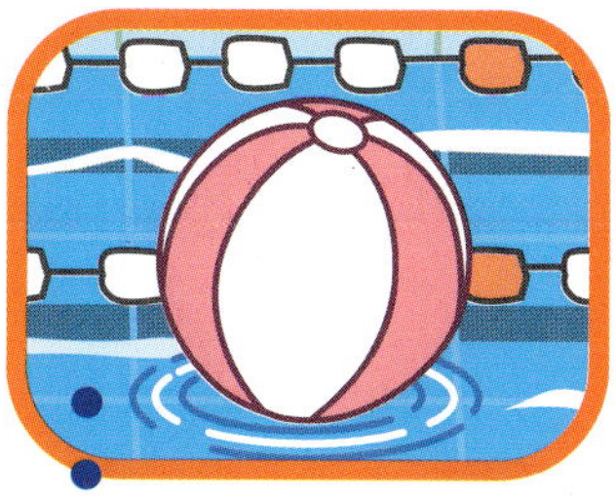
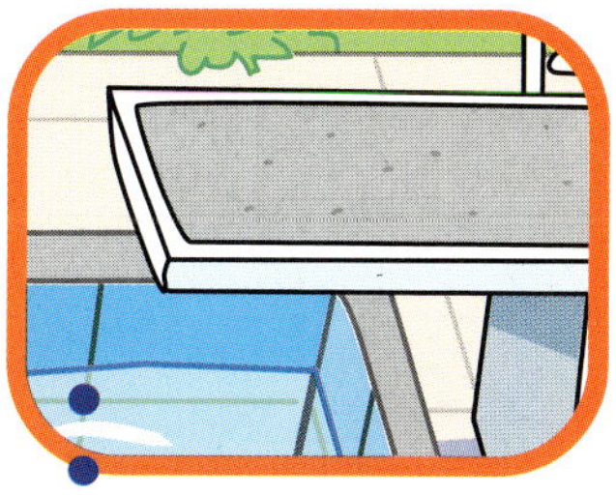

der Wasserball
water ball

das Sprungbrett
springboard

die Trillerpfeife
whistle

das Badelaken
bath towel

der Badeschuh
bathing shoe

der Schlüssel
key

der Startblock
starting block

Ein Tag mit der Maus

A day with the Mouse

Gute Nacht, Maus! Schlaf schön!

Good night, Mouse! Sleep tight!

Am Nachmittag skaten die Maus, der Elefant und die Ente.

In the afternoon, the Mouse, the Elephant and the Duck are skating.

Die Maus und der Elefant ruhen sich aus und betrachten die Wolken.

The Mouse and the Elephant are having a rest. They are looking at the clouds.

Guten Morgen!
Die Maus und ihre Freunde frühstücken.

Good morning! The Mouse and its friends are having breakfast.

Die Maus, der Elefant und die Ente spielen im Kindergarten.

The Mouse, the Elephant and the Duck are playing in the nursery.

Die Maus und ihre Freunde machen Obstsalat für das Mittagessen.

The Mouse and its friends are preparing fruit salad for lunch.

Farben
Colours

die Staffelei
easel

die Leinwand
canvas

der Pinsel
brush

die Farbtube
tube of paint

der Farbtopf
paint pot

grün
green

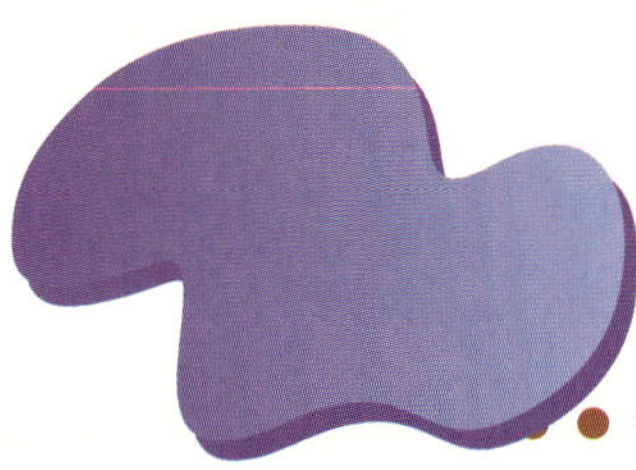

lila
purple

Oh nein! Orange für das Herbstbild ist leider nicht mehr da. Aus welchen zwei Farben kann die Maus Orange mischen?

Oh dear! There is no orange left for the autumn picture. Which two colours can the mouse mix to make orange?

Lösung: Gelb und Rot.
Answer: yellow and red.

Tennis-Spiel

A game of tennis

der Kegel
skittle

der Schlittschuh
ice skate

der Helm
helmet

der Tennisball
tennis ball

der Tennisschläger
tennis racket

der Rollschuh
roller skate

der Turnschuh
trainer

das Schweißband
sweat band

die Schirmmütze
cap

der Schwimmring
swim ring

der Boxhandschuh
boxing glove

Maus und Elefant wollen Tennis spielen. Welche Gegenstände brauchen sie? Wähle aus.

The Mouse and the Elephant want to play tennis. Which of these things do they need?

Lösung: Die Maus und der Elefant brauchen den Tennisschläger, den Tennisball, die Turnschuhe und die Schweißbänder.

Answer: The Mouse and the Elephant need the tennis racket, the tennis ball, the trainers and the sweat bands.

Wie fühlst du dich?

How do you feel?

Die Maus ist wütend.
The Mouse is angry.

Die Maus ist traurig.
The Mouse is sad.

Die Maus ist ratlos.
The Mouse is at a loss.

Die Ente ist verdutzt.
The duck is puzzled.

Die Maus ist vergnügt.
The Mouse is happy.

Die Maus ist erfreut.
The Mouse is pleased.

Gute Nacht!
Good night!

die Taschenlampe
torch

die Nachttischlampe
bedside lamp

der Nachttisch
bedside table

das Buch
book

der Mond
moon
der Vorhang
curtain
das Fenster
window
die Bettdecke
duvet
das Bett
bed
die Schlafmütze
night cap
der Hausschuh
slipper
der Basketball
basketball
das Auto
car

Wörterverzeichnis

List of Words

A

Abfalleimer – bin [bɪn]
acht – eight [eɪt]
Adler – eagle [ˈiːgl]
Affe – monkey [ˈmʌŋkɪ]
Ameise – ant [ænt]
Ananas – pineapple [ˈpaɪnˌæpl]
angeln – (to) fish [tuː fɪʃ]
Apfel – apple [ˈæpl]
April – April [ˈeɪprəl]
auf – at / on [ˈæt] / [ɒn]
Arm – arm [ɑːm]
Armbanduhr – wrist watch [ˈrɪst ˈwɒːtʃ]
Ast – branch [brɑːntʃ]
Auge – eye [aɪ]
August – August [ˈɔːgəst]
ausmalen – (to) colour [tuː kʌləʳ]
ausruhen – (to) (have a) rest [tuː hæv ə rest]
ausschneiden – (to) cut out [tuː kʌt aʊt]
Auto – car [kɑːʳ]
Autoreifen – car tyre [kɑːʳ taɪəʳ]

B

Badelaken – bath towel [bɑːθ ˈtaʊəl]
Badeschuh – bathing shoe [ˈbeɪðɪŋ ʃuː]
Badezimmer – bathroom [ˈbɑːθruːm]
Ball – ball [bɔːl]
Banane – banana [bəˈnɑːnə]
Basketball – basketball [bɑːskɪtbɔːl]
Bauen – (to) build [tuː bɪld]
Baum – tree [triː]
Becher – cup [kʌp]
Beet – flower bed [ˈflaʊəʳ bed]
bei – with [wɪθ, wɪð]
Bein – leg [leg]
Besen – broom [bruːm]
betrachten – (to) look at [tuː lʊk æt]
Bett – bed [bed]
Bettdecke – duvet [ˈduːveɪ]
Bild – picture [ˈpɪktʃəʳ]
Bildwörterbuch – picture dictionary [ˈpɪktʃəʳ ˈdɪkʃənərɪ]
Birne – pear [pɛəʳ]
Blatt – leaf [ˈliːf]
blau – blue [ˈbluː]
Blume – flower [ˈflaʊəʳ]
Blumentopf – flower pot [ˈflaʊəʳ pɒt]
Boxhandschuh – boxing glove [bɒksɪŋ glʌv]
brauchen – (to) need [tuː niːd]
braun – brown [braʊn]
Brot – bread [bred]
Brücke – bridge [ˈbrɪdʒ]
Brustbeutel – pouch [ˈpaʊtʃ]
Buch – book [bʊk]
Bus – bus [ˈbʌs]
Butter – butter [ˈbʌtəʳ]
Butterbrot – sandwich [ˈsænwɪdʒ]

C

Clown – clown [klaʊn]

D

das/der/die – the [ðə, vor Vokalen auch ðiː]
Decke – blanket [ˈblæŋkɪt]
deutsch – German [ˈdʒɜːmən]
Dezember – December [dɪˈsembəʳ]
diese/dieser/dieses – this [ðɪs]
drei – three [θriː]
du – you [juː]

E

Ei – egg [eg]
Eimer – bucket [bʌkɪt]
eins – one [wʌn]
Eisenbahn – train [ˈtreɪn]
Elefant – elephant [ˈelɪfənt]
englisch – English [ˈɪŋglɪʃ]
Ente – duck [dʌk]
erfreut – pleased [ˈpliːzd]

F

fangen – (to) catch [tuː kætʃ]
Farbe – colour [ˈkʌləʳ]
Farbtopf – paint pot [peɪnt pɒt]
Farbtube – tube of paint [tjuːb əv peɪnt]
Februar – February [ˈfebrʊərɪ]
Fenster – window [ˈwɪndəʊ]
finden – (to) find / (to) spot [tuː faɪnd] / [tuː spɒt]
Fisch – fish [fɪʃ]
Flasche – bottle [ˈbɒtl]
Floß – raft [rɑːft]
Floß fahren – (to) float on a raft [tuː fləʊt ɒn ə rɑːft]
folgen – (to) follow [tuː ˈfɒləʊ]
Förmchen – sand mould [sænd məʊld]
Freund – friend [frend]
Frühling – spring [sprɪŋ]
frühstücken – (to) have breakfast [tuː hæv ˈbrekfəst]
fühlen – (to) feel [tuː fiːl]
fünf – five [faɪv]
für – for [fɔːʳ]
Fußball – soccer [ˈsɒkəʳ]

G

Gabel – fork [fɔːk]
Garten – garden [ˈgɑːdn]
Gegenstand – thing [θɪŋ]
gehören – (to) belong to [tuː bɪlɒŋ tuː]
gelb – yellow [ˈjeləʊ]
gern haben/machen/mögen – (to) like / (to) love [tuː laɪk] / [tuː lʌv]
gewinnen – (to) win [tuː wɪn]

Gießkanne – watering can [wɔ:tɜ:ɪŋ kæn]
Giraffe – giraffe [dʒɪˈrɑ:f]
Gitarre – guitar [gɪˈtɑʳ]
Glas – glass [glɑ:s]
Glockenspiel – glockenspiel [ˈglɒkənspi:l]
Golf – golf [gɒlf]
Gräte – fish bone [fɪʃ bəʊn]
grillen – (to) have a barbecue [tu: hæv ə ˈbɑ:bɪkju:]
grün – green [gri:n]
Gurke – cucumber [ˈkju:kʌmbəʳ]
gut – good [gʊd]

H

Hamster – hamster [hæmstəʳ]
Handschuh – glove [glʌv]
Handtuch – towel [taʊəl]
Hase – hare [hɛəʳ]
Hausschuh – slipper [ˈslɪpəʳ]
helfen – (to) help [tu: help]
Helm – helmet [ˈhelmɪt]
herausfinden – (to) find out [tu: faɪnd aʊt]
Herbst – autumn [ˈɔ:təm]
Himmel – sky [skaɪ]
hinter – behind [bɪˈhaɪnd]
Honig – honey [ˈhʌnɪ]
hören – (to) listen [tu: lɪsn]
Huhn – chicken [ˈtʃɪkɪn]
Hühnerbein – chicken leg [ˈtʃɪkɪn leg]
Hund – dog [dɒg]

I

ihr/ihre – its [ɪts]
im/in – in [ɪn]
Inlineskate – inline skate [ɪnlaɪn skeɪt]

J

Jahreszeit – season [ˈsi:zn]
Januar – January [ˈdʒænjʊərɪ]
Judo – judo [ˈdʒu:dəʊ]
Juli – July [dʒu:ˈlaɪ]
Juni – June [dʒu:n]

K

Kamm – comb [kəʊm]
Karotte – carrot [ˈkærət]
Kartoffel – potato [pəˈteɪtəʊ]
Käse – cheese [tʃi:z]
Katze – cat [kæt]
Kegel – skittle [ˈskɪtl]
kennen – (to) know [tu: nəʊ]
Kindergarten – nursery [ˈnɜ:sərɪ]
Kirsche – cherry [ˈtʃerɪ]
Kissen – pillow [ˈpɪləʊ]
Kiste – box [bɒks]
Klettergerüst – climbing frame [ˈklaɪmɪŋ freɪm]
Klopapier – toilet paper [ˈtɔɪlɪt ˈpeɪpəʳ]
können – (to) can [tu: kæn]
Kontrabass – double bass [ˈdʌbl beɪs]
Korb – basket [ˈbɑ:skɪt]
Kraft – strength [streŋθ]
Krokodil – crocodile [ˈkrɒkədaɪl]
Küche – kitchen [ˈkɪtʃɪn]
Kuchen – cake [keɪk]

L

Lampe – lamp [læmp]
legen – (to) lay [tu: laɪ]
Leiter – ladder [ˈlædəʳ]
Leinwand – canvas [ˈkænvəs]
lernen – (to) learn [tu: lɜ:n]
lesen – (to) read [tu: ri:d]
lila – purple [ˈpɜ:pl]
Linie – line [laɪn]
Lösung – answer [ˈɑ:nsəʳ]
Luftballon – balloon [bəˈlu:n]

M

machen – (to) do [tu: du:]
Mai – May [meɪ]
Marmelade – jam [dʒæm]
März – March [mɑ:tʃ]
Maus – mouse [maʊs]
Mantel – coat [ˈkəʊt]
Melone (runder Hut) – bowler hat [ˈbəʊlɜ: ˈhæt]
Messer – knife [naɪf]
Meterbrot – bread stick [bred stɪk]
Milch – milk [mɪlk]
mischen – (to) mix [tu: mɪks]
mit – with [wɪð, wɪθ]
mitbringen – (to) bring [tu: brɪŋ]
Mittagessen – lunch [lʌntʃ]
Mond – moon [mu:n]
Morgen – morning [ˈmɔ:nɪŋ]
Musik – music [ˈmju:zɪk]
musizieren – (to) play music [tu: pleɪ ˈmju:zɪk]
Mütze – woolly hat [ˈwʊlɪ hæt]

N

Nachmittag – afternoon [ˈɑ:ftəˈnu:n]
Nacht – night [naɪt]
Nachttisch – bedside table [ˈbedsaɪd ˈteɪbl]
Nachttischlampe – bedside lamp [ˈbedsaɪd læmp]
Nashorn – rhinoceros [raɪˈnɒsərəs]
neben – next to [nekst tu:]
neun – nine [naɪn]
Nilpferd – hippopotamus [ˌhɪpəˈpɒtəməs]
November – November [nəʊˈvembəʳ]

O

Obstsalat – fruit salad [fru:t ˈsæləd]
Ohr – ear [ɪəʳ]
Oktober – October [ɒkˈtəʊbəʳ]
Orange – orange [ˈɒrɪndʒ]
Orangenscheibe – orange slice [ˈɒrɪndʒ slaɪs]

P

Paar – pair [pɛəʳ]
packen – (to) pack [tu: pæk]
Parfum – perfume [ˈpɜ:fju:m]
pflanzen – (to) plant [tu: plɑ:nt]
pflücken – (to) pick [tu: pɪk]
Picknick – picnic [ˈpɪknɪk]
Pilz – mushroom [ˈmʌʃrʊm]
Pinsel – brush [brʌʃ]

Q

Quietsche-Ente – rubber duck [ˈrʌbəʳ dʌk]

R

Rasen – lawn [lɔ:n]
Rasenmäher – lawnmower [lɔ:nˈməʊəʳ]
ratlos – at a loss [æt ə lɒs]
Regenbogen – rainbow [ˈreɪnbəʊ]
Rettungsring – rescue ring [ˈreskju: rɪŋ]

Ring – ring [rɪŋ]
Ritter – knight [naɪt]
Ritterrüstung – armour ['ɑ:məʳ]
Roller – scooter ['sku:təʳ]
Rollschuh – roller skate ['rəʊləʳ skeɪt]
rosa – pink [pɪŋk]
rot – red [red]
Rucksack – rucksack ['rʌksæk]
Rüssel – trunk [trʌŋk]
Rutsche – slide [slaɪd]

S

Sandkiste – sand box [sænd bɒks]
Schal – scarf [skɑ:f]
Schaufel – shovel [ʃʌvl]
Schild – shield [ʃi:ld]
Schirm – umbrella [ə'mbrɛlə]
Schirmmütze – cap [kæp]
schlafen – (to) sleep [tu: sli:p]
Schlafmütze – night cap [naɪt kæp]
Schlittschuh – ice skate [aɪs skert]
Schlüssel – key [ki:]
Schmetterling – butterfly ['bʌtəflaɪ]
Schnabel – beak [bi:k]
Schnauze – muzzle ['mʌzl]
Schneemann – snowman [snəʊmæn]
Schuh – shoe [ʃu:]
Schwanz – tail [teɪl]
schwarz – black [blæk]
Schwebebalken – balance beam ['bæləns 'bi:m]
Schwert – sword [sɔ:d]
Schweißband – sweat band [swet bænd]
Schwimmbad – swimming pool ['swɪmɪŋ pu:l]
schwimmen – (to) swim [tu: swɪm]
Schwimmring – swim ring [swɪm rɪŋ]
sechs – six [sɪks]
sehen – (to) see [tu: si:]
sein – (to) be [tu: bi:]
September – September [sep'tembəʳ]
sie – they [ðeɪ]
sieben – seven ['sevn]
sitzen – (to) sit [tu: sɪt]
skaten – (to) skate [tu: skeɪt]
Ski – ski [ski:]
Ski laufen – (to) ski [tu: ski:]
Sommer – summer ['sʌməʳ]
Spaghetti – spaghetti [spə'getɪ]
Spaß – fun [fʌn]
Spaten – spade [speɪd]
Spiegel – mirror ['mɪrəʳ]
Spiel – game [geɪm]
spielen – (to) play [tu: pleɪ]
Spielkarte – card [kɑ:d]
Spielplatz – playground [pleɪgraʊnd]
Spielzeug – toy [tɔɪ]
Sport – sport [spɔ:t]
springen – (to) jump [tu: dʒʌmp]
Sprungbrett – springboard ['sprɪŋbɔ:d]
Staffelei – easel ['i:zl]
Startblock – starting block ['stɑ:tɪŋ blɒk]
stehen – (to) stand [tu: stænd]
Stern – star [stɑ:ʳ]

T

Tag – day [deɪ]
Taschenlampe – torch [tɔ:tʃ]
tauchen – (to) dive [tu: daɪv]
Tennis – tennis ['tenɪs]
Tennisball – tennis ball ['tenɪs bɔ:l]
Tennisschläger – tennis racket ['tenɪs 'rækɪt]
Teddybär – teddy bear ['tedɪ ˌbɛəʳ]
Teller – plate [pleɪt]
Tier – animal ['ænɪməl]
Tisch – table ['teɪbl]
Tomate – tomato [tə'mɒtəʊ]
traurig – sad [sæd]
Trillerpfeife – whistle ['wɪsl]
Trinkflasche – flask [flɑ:sk]
turnen – (to) exercise [tu: 'eksəsaɪz]
Turnschuh – trainer ['treɪnəʳ]

U

Uhr – clock [klɒk]
und – and [ænd, ənd]
unter – under ['ʌndəʳ]
Unterschied – difference ['dɪfrəns]

V

verdutzt – puzzled ['pʌzld]
vergnügt – happy ['hæpɪ]
verkleiden – (to) dress up [tu: dres ʌp]
verschießen – (to) kick away [tu: kɪk ə'weɪ]
verstecken – (to) hide [tu: haɪd]
viel – many ['menɪ]
vier – four [fɔ:ʳ]
Vogel – bird [bɜ:d]
Vogelscheuche – scarecrow [skɛəʳkrəʊ]
vor – in front of [ɪn frʌnt əf]
Vorhang – curtain ['kɜ:tn]

W

warten – (to) wait [tu: weɪt]
was – what [wɒt]
Waschbecken – washbasin ['wɒʃbeɪsən]
Wasserball – water ball ['wɔ:təʳ bɔ:l]
Wasserhahn – tap ['tæp]
weiß – white [waɪt]
weit – far [fɑ:ʳ]
Weitspringen – long jump [lɒŋ dʒʌmp]
wer – who [hu:]
wie – how [haʊ]
Wiese – meadow ['medəʊ]
Windmühle – windmill ['wɪndmɪl]
Winter – winter ['wɪntəʳ]
wo – where [wɛəʳ]
Wolke – cloud [klaʊd]
wollen – (to) want [tu: wɒnt]
Wörterverzeichnis – list of words [lɪst əv wɜ:dz]
Wurst – sausage ['sɒsɪdʒ]
wütend – angry ['æŋgrɪ]

Z

zählen – (to) count [tu: kaʊnt]
Zahnbürste – toothbrush [tu:θbrʌʃ]
Zahnpasta – toothpaste [tu:θpeɪst]
zaubern – (to) do magic tricks [tu: du: 'mædʒɪk trɪkz]
zehn – ten [ten]
zwei – two [tu:]
zwischen – between [bɪ'twi:n]

Finde die Paare!

Find the pairs!

Schneide die Spielkarten aus und lege sie mit den Bildern nach unten auf den Tisch. Kannst du die Kartenpaare finden?

Cut out the cards and lay them face down on the table. Can you find the pairs of matching cards?